RHYTHM BLUES

by ROBBEN FORD

PERFORMED BY ROBBEN FORD

Mix and Editing . . . . Don Mock
Audio Engineer . . . . Daniel G. Cantor
Music Engraving . . . . Glenn D. Greenwood
Audio Recording . . . . Firstake, Inc.
Audio Mixing . . . . American Production Services
Executive Producer . . . . Roger Hutchinson

To access audio visit:
www.halleonard.com/mylibrary

Enter Code
2147-8402-7066-1682

Cover photo by William Hames

ISBN 978-0-7935-2754-0

HAL•LEONARD®

Visit Hal Leonard Online at
www.halleonard.com

Contact us:
Hal Leonard
7777 West Bluemound Road
Milwaukee, WI 53213
Email: info@halleonard.com

In Europe, contact:
Hal Leonard Europe Limited
42 Wigmore Street
Marylebone, London, W1U 2RN
Email: info@halleonardeurope.com

In Australia, contact:
Hal Leonard Australia Pty. Ltd.
4 Lentara Court
Cheltenham, Victoria, 3192 Australia
Email: info@halleonard.com.au

EXAMPLE 1

INTRO

C7

F7   C7

G7   F7

INTRO/ENDING

FUNKY BLUES

EXAMPLE 2

TRACK 4

INTRO

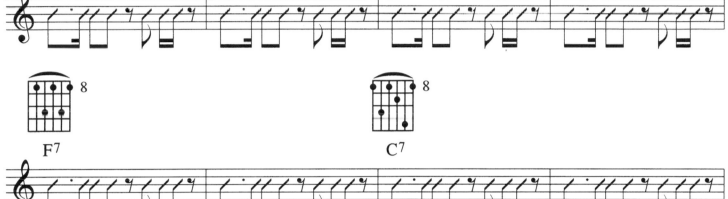

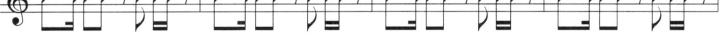

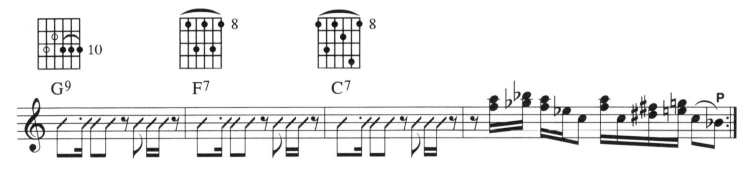

INTRO/ENDING

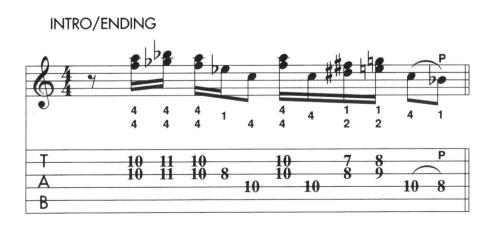

EXAMPLE 3

TRACK 5

Funky Blues

Example 4

🔊 **Track 6**

MASTER RHYTHM

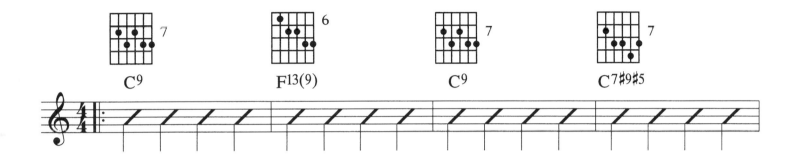

C^9 $F^{13(9)}$ C^9 $C^{7\sharp9\sharp5}$

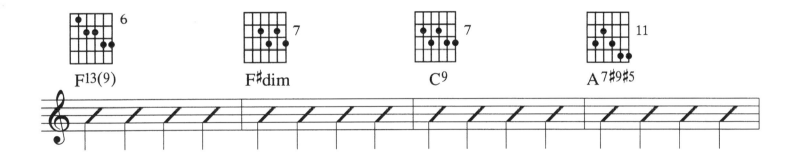

$F^{13(9)}$ $F\sharp dim$ C^9 $A^{7\sharp9\sharp5}$

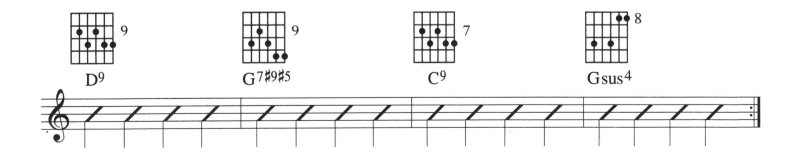

D^9 $G^{7\sharp9\sharp5}$ C^9 $Gsus^4$

EXAMPLE 1

🔊 **TRACK 7**

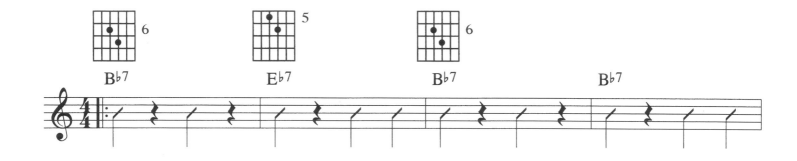

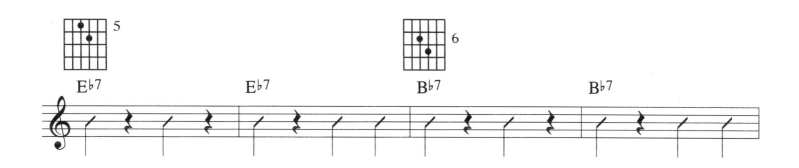

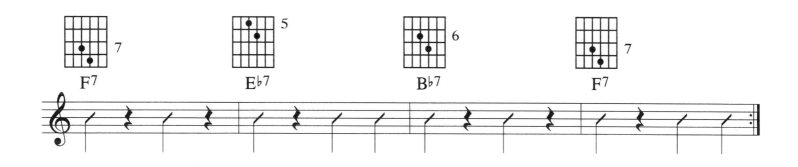

SHUFFLE BLUES

EXAMPLE 2

🔊 TRACK 8

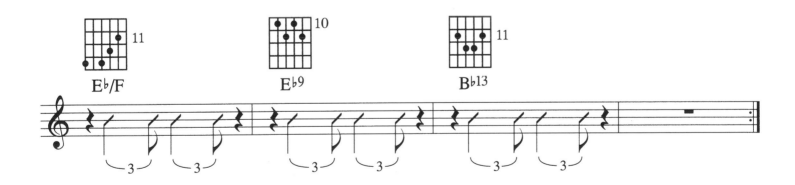

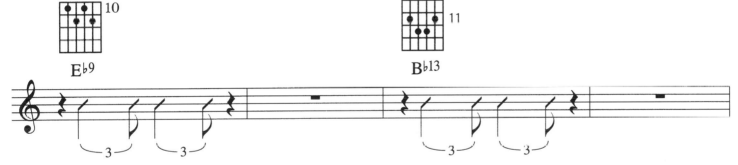

EXAMPLE 3

🔊 TRACK 9

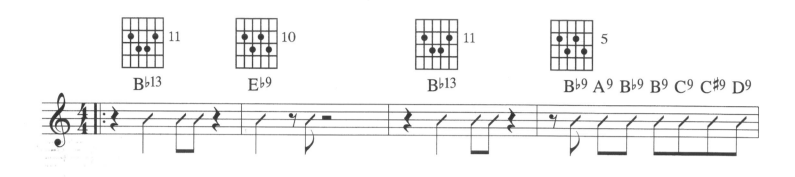

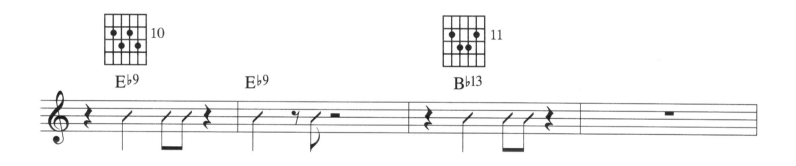

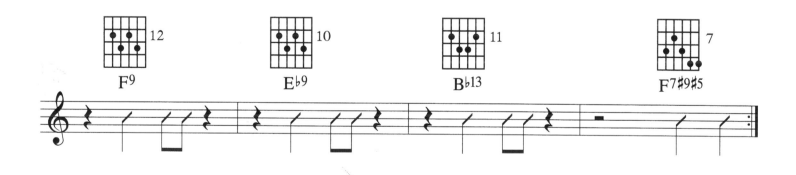

SHUFFLE BLUES

EXAMPLE 4

🔊 TRACK 10

INTRO

COMP

EXAMPLE 5

🔊 **TRACK 11**

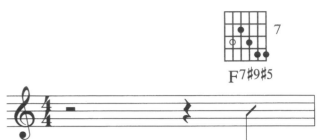

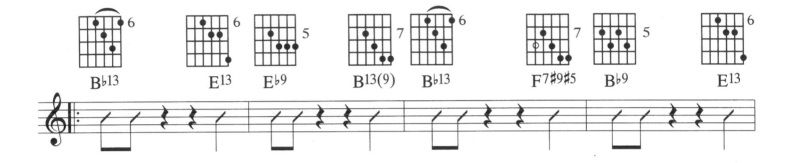

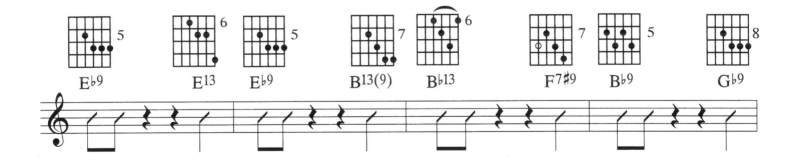

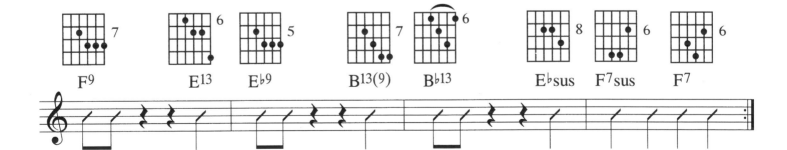

SHUFFLE BLUES

EXAMPLE 6

🔊 TRACK 12

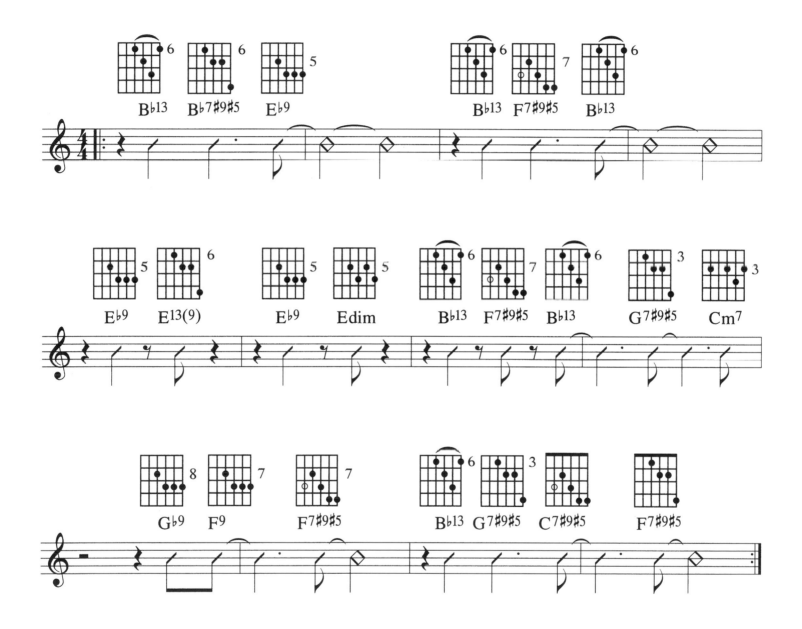

11

EXAMPLE 7

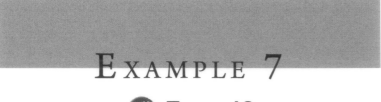

🔊 TRACK 13

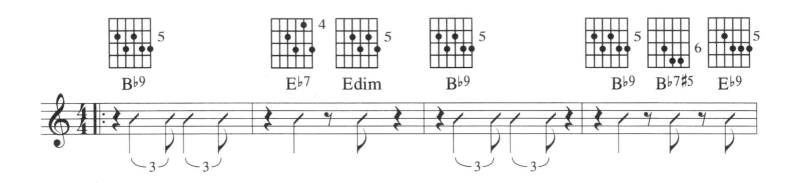

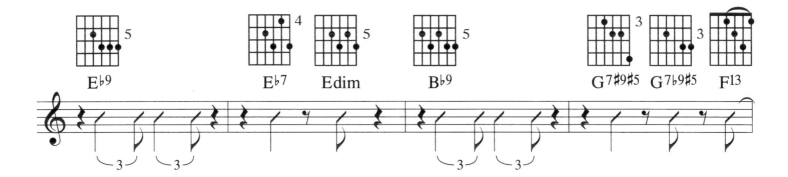

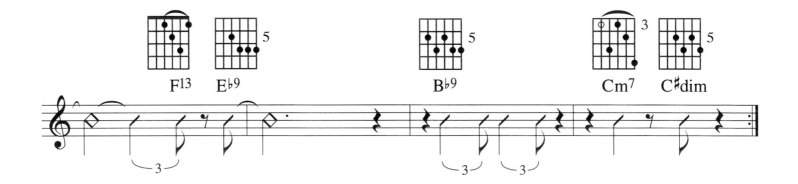

Slow Blues

Example 1

Track 14

fingerings and articulations - simile

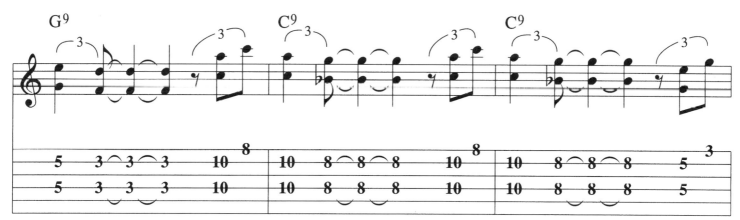

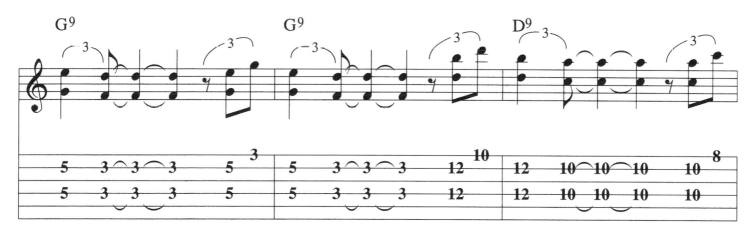

13

EXAMPLE 2

TRACK 15

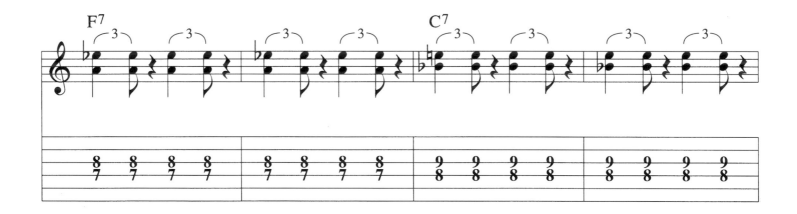

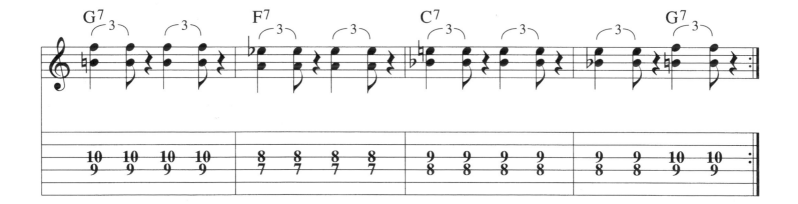

Slow Blues

Example 3

TRACK 16

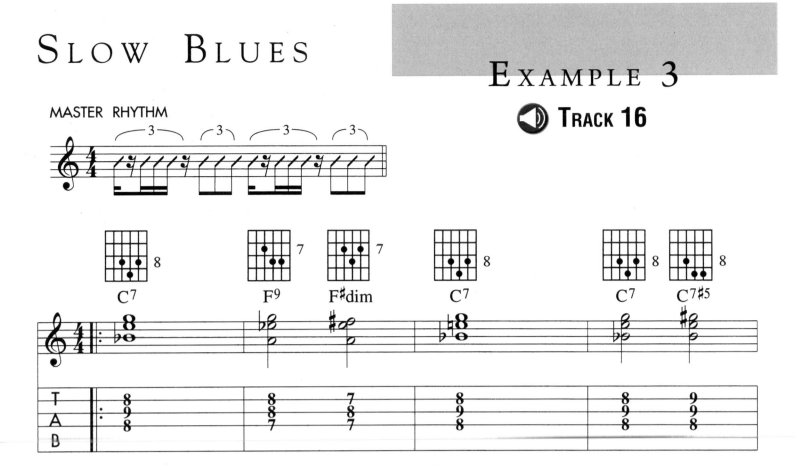

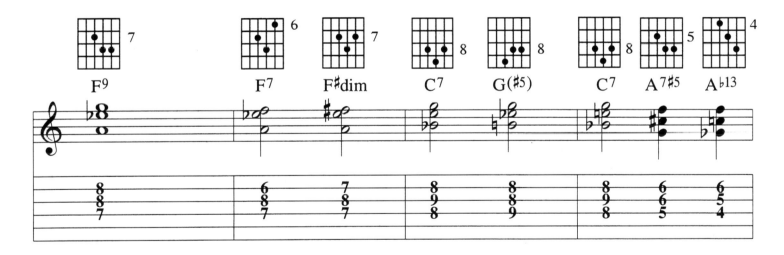

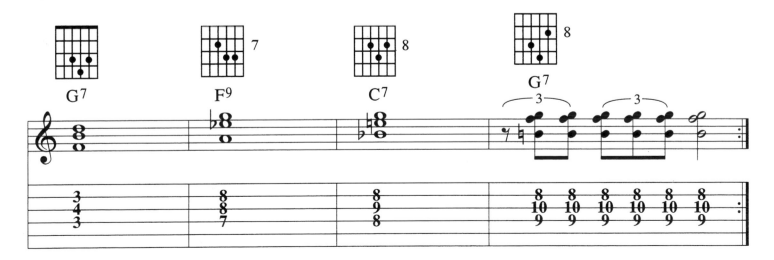

EXAMPLES 4 & 5

TRACK 17

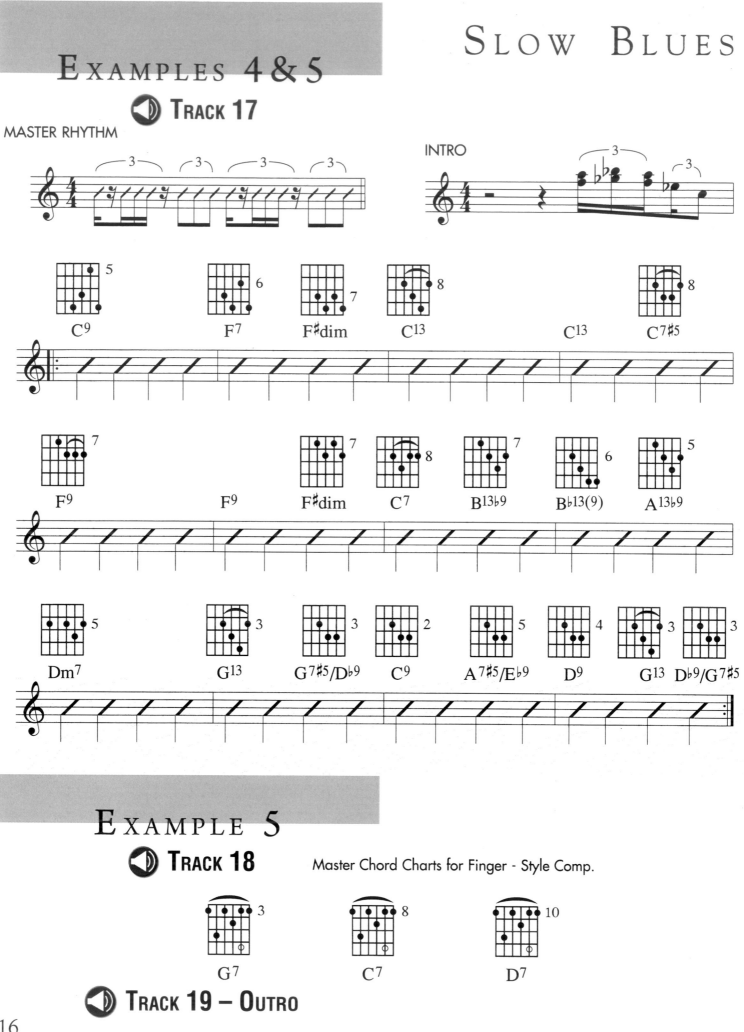

MASTER RHYTHM

INTRO

C9 F7 F#dim C13 C13 C7#5

F9 F9 F#dim C7 B13b9 Bb13(9) A13b9

Dm7 G13 G7#5/Db9 C9 A7#5/Eb9 D9 G13 Db9/G7#5

EXAMPLE 5

TRACK 18   Master Chord Charts for Finger - Style Comp.

G7 C7 D7

TRACK 19 – OUTRO